Dear reader,

It is my sincere hope that book will help you with your roofing project. But if you do find yourself overwhelmed there is nothing wrong with reaching out and asking for help.

You can reach me at

prcofarizona@gmail.com

I am here to help as best as I can.

Thanks

How to Find, Hire and Work with a Roofing Contractor

(or any contractor)

By

Henry Staggs

Roof Consultant

Preferred Roof Consultants of Arizona, LLC.

Chandler Arizona

How to Find, Hire and Work with a Roofing Contractor

(or any contractor)

By

Henry Staggs

Published by

Preferred Roof Consultants of Arizona, LLC.

Chandler Arizona

Copyright © 2016 By Henry Staggs

First Edition 2016

Dedicated to Robert Spicklemire

This book is dedicated to my old school friend Robert. His advice to me when I was starting out in this business so many years ago still rings true in my ears. It has influenced my career ever since. He gave me the following words of wisdom.

"Read the directions, they 're right there on the package, dumb ass."

I am sad to say that Robert is no longer with us, but his memory is alive and to this very day I am still hearing his voice in my head. Reminding me to follow the directions.

Legal Disclaimer

Table of Contents

About the Author

Henry Staggs is seasoned roofer and roofing contractor. Henry started his long career in roofing in 1981, helping his grandfather with his rental homes. Being one of the few kids willing to get on the roof, Henry found himself doing most of his grandfather's roof repair jobs.

By his early 20's Henry was running a company working as a sub-contractor. Henry also did some contracting work on the military base located next door to his home town. He as been the sub-contractor, the prime contractor. Worked on government projects, worked on restoration jobs, worked on insurance jobs and pretty much any other kinds of jobs you can think of.

Henry has worked in three difference states over the years, and has hands on experience with most types of residential and commercial roofing systems.

Henry has owned three different roofing companies, and two handyman companies. Henry has always strives to learn and grown in his industry. It seemed natural for Henry to transition from roofer, to roofing contractor to roof consultant.

How to use this book

After spending several years focusing my roofing work on repairs almost exclusively, I have learned a great many things about the mistakes that so many contractors make over and over. Not just by doing repairs, but also having inspected hundreds of roofs over the past several years. I see the same problems again and again.

Why is this? My theory is very simple. The roofers are doing what they have always done. And when a leak does develop either the contractor is long gone or you're past the two-year time period that the ROC will accept the complaint. So they ignore you or blame you for anything else other than the work.

The sad fact is that more than half of the new roofs installed this year will leak within the first five years.

This book was written to help you avoid being one of those people with a NEW LEAKING roof. Imagine paying thousands of dollars for a new roof. Only for it to leak within the first five years.

This book will help you

- Find a qualified contractor

- Hire that contractor

- Make sure that your new roof is installed correctly

- Not get ripped off

What you will need

- A computer with Internet access

- A printer or access to a printer

- A copier or access to a copier

- A job folder for all the documents that you will be collecting

- pens

- this book

The advice in this book is simple and to the point. Read each page and take notes. If you have questions, write them down. There will be some learning involved. Use the worksheets in the back of the book to help you along the way.

HAPPY ROOFING

Roofing in Arizona

It's a fact that in Arizona it does not rain very often. But when it does, we get a lot of it in a very short amount of time. What does that mean for roofs in Arizona? Well, since it does not rain year round, it means that leaks can go undetected for a long time. Sometimes even years.

Keep in mind that before you see the leak inside your home, the water had to travel through the roof, and the insulation in your attic. And then finally through your drywall and paint. Since it gets hot in Arizona, the water may evaporate before it makes it all the way to your interior. Making the leak and the damage worse each time it rains. Eventually, given the right conditions it will make its way to the interior and you notice that you have a leak.

This is also why there is usually wood damage associated with roof leaks in Arizona. The leak may have gone undetected for some time, each time wetting the wood. Then it dries up and then gets wet again. Each time damaging the wood.

We can't put all the blame on the weather though. Our unique weather patterns make leaks more elusive. However, the root of the problem is more often than not, in the installation. It was simply installed wrong. You won't know that until you see the leak inside. Of course there are always exceptions to the rule. And if the problem is a big one you will probably notice it much sooner. But most of the time they are small leaks that slowly damage your home over time.

Some other roof problems that I have seen in Arizona are: birds, insects, and plants. The birds will build their nest in your roof and "poop" everywhere. Not only is this a health hazard for you and your family, it destroys roofing materials. I have seen bees build their hives in roofs, making a very stick mess. I have seen carpenter bees and termites eat away the wood. I have seen plants growing on and into the roof. All of these thing destroy the roofing materials and cause expensive damage.

When you do see a leak, chances are good that we have just been through a rainy cycle. You call a contractor, and they are busy. You call another and they are busy, and so on. Until finally you find someone who can come out and look at your roof problem. Thanks to supply and demand, they charge you a very nice penny to do the repairs. Since you have no other choice you hire them and cross your fingers that they actually fix the problem. Who knows when we will get enough rain to find out?

That is why I decided to write this book. And why I have dedicated the second half my working life to roof consulting. I have repaired far too many roofs to sit by and say nothing. With a few small changes and some homework on your part most roof problems can be easily avoided. If almost all roof leaks in Arizona are due to poor installation, then it seems reasonable to me that the solution is to do it right the first time.

You could consider hiring a roof consultant to help you. A good roof consultant is well worth the fee that they charge. However, if you choose to go it on your own, this book will help to make sure that you find, hire and work with a qualified roofing contractor.

Who is the ROC?

Their mission

Quoting the ROC's website: *"To promote quality construction by Arizona contractors through a licensing and regulatory system to protect the health, safety, and welfare of the public."*

Let's talk about who the ROC is

I will summarize who the ROC is here; but I urge you to visit their website. It offers a treasure trove of information. The ROC is a truly great resource.

The Arizona legislature established the Registrar of Contractors in 1931. Their role is to regulate both the commercial and residential construction industries, by investigating and helping to resolve complaints made against licensed and unlicensed contractors.

Who pays for the ROC?

The ROC is not a taxpayer supported agency. The ROC is funded 100% by contractor's fees. Ten percent of those fees go to the state's general fund. The ROC is not a burden on the taxpayers, while contributing to the state's general fund.

What can the ROC do for you?

At their site you can find many articles written to help you find, hire and work with a contractor. Tips and advice that will help you avoid getting ripped off. You can find a list the "most wanted" bad contractors on their site. You can also check a contractor's licensing status, and learn pretty much anything you want to know about contracting in Arizona.

Protecting You

The ROC requires that all contractors carry a bond. Additionally, their "recovery fund" is also available. Both are in place to help homeowners recover any cost they may incur when a contractor does a bad job, or does not finish a job.

We will talk more about bonds and the recovery fund later in the section on "Handling a problem."

To summarize, the ROC is your friend! But they are not a ratings site. They don't care if you don't like the contractor's attitude, or customer service skills. They do care if the contractor is doing their work below standard or doesn't finish at all.

I strongly recommend you take some time now, before reading on, to visit their site and become familiar with how to navigate it, and what they have to offer.

www.azroc.gov

Finding a good roofing contractor

"Good help is so hard to find" - every employer in history.

Believe me it's true! Over the years that I have been a contractor I have learned that finding good help is like finding a diamond in a pile of coal. You would be very close in saying that 1 of 100 workers is "good help". Any contractor who can attract and keep good workers has my respect.

You are looking for a good contractor. Why else would you be reading this book? I have no delusion that anyone would read my book for fun so let's get started on finding a good contractor for you.

In my humble opinion a good contractor is one who can get the job done for the amount of money agreed to in a reasonable amount of time. As you work through this book, you will learn which contractors meet these standards, which ones do not and most importantly which one you want to work with. Use the "Finding a contractor" worksheet to help start collecting data and narrowing down your list. (see "worksheets")

Family and friends

Start your search for a good contractor close to home. Ask your family, friends, neighbors, co-workers, business associates and so on, if they know any good contractors. Chances are very good that some of them do know a good contractor.

As you get names of contractors, write them in on your, "Finding a contractor" worksheet. If you have their phone number write that in too. However, at this point that isn't vital, you will be gathering more information on them as you go. For now you just want names.

Signs

Contractors pay good money for colorful signs on their trucks and in the yards of their customers. You might see a truck somewhere, or perhaps there is work going on in your neighborhood.

If you see a truck or a yard sign that grabs your attention, write down that contractor's name on your "Finding a contractor" worksheet. Since you are looking at a sign you will probably see a phone number, website and ROC number as well. Write all that down on your "Finding a contractor" worksheet.

NOTE Arizona law requires that a contractor always include their ROC number on any and all advertisements.

The Internet, the great equalizer

Social media

In the same way that you ask your family and friends for good contractors, post your request on any social media site you are part of. Seems that today most people are on social media sites every day. You will probably get several recommendations.

As you get more names of contractors, write them in on your "Finding a contractor" worksheet. However, at this point that isn't vital, you will be gathering more information on them as you go.

Search engine

Of course, you can always search for contractors online, using terms like "Arizona roofer" or "Roof replacement" or "Roof repairs" or "Roofer" and the name of your city. Keep in mind that the contractors on the front page aren't necessarily better contractors. Better at Internet marketing perhaps, but they may be as good (or not) as another contractor five pages in. Don't limit your search to just one page.

As you get names of contractors, write them in on your "Finding a contractor" worksheet. If you have their phone number, write that in too.

Certified contractors

I am going to share with you a few really cool tips on finding contractors. Assuming that you know what kind of roof you have, or want to have, find a manufacturer who supplies your area. Any supplier can give you a few names. Go to their websites and find their certified contractor's search link. Most of them have some sort of contractor certification/referral program.

Contractors who take the time to be certified by a manufacturer show that they take their business seriously. There are extra hoops to jump through, extra costs and often fees to become a certified contractor.

As you get names of contractors, write them in on your "Finding a contractor" worksheet.

Trade associations

Another great way to find good contractors is through industry trade associations. To be a member of a trade association the contractor has to agree to their standards. They must be insured and licensed. And pay extra fees each year, which can be as steep as a thousand dollars or more.

Just as with the contractor certification programs, these contractors show that they take their business seriously, and that they are participating in the industry itself. Not just trying to make money on it.

As you get names of contractors, write them in on your "Finding a contractor" worksheet. If you have their phone number, write that in too.

Shingles

GAF, Malarkey, Owens Corning, Certainteed

Tile

Boral, Eagle Roofing Products, Redland Clay Tile

Metal

ABC American Building Components, ASC Building Products

(There are many more manufacturers, this is a very small list)

Roof Associations

(there are many others, this is a very short list)

www.azroofing.org www.nrca.net www.wsrca.com

www.tileroofing.org www.metalroofing.com

Looking up the contractor's license

As I was working on my final draft of this book, I received an email from the ROC, telling me that they are redesigning their website. Suggesting that I should wait a few months to complete the book.

This means that the entire section that I wrote about navigating the ROC's site, could be rendered useless. Discouraging at first, but when I thought about it, I decided it's good news after all.

I've re-written this section to help guide you. Even though it won't be the step-by step guide that I intended, it will still provide you with more than enough information to make good use of the ROC's website, when reviewing a contractor's license history.

This is where your real work begins. Finding a contractor takes time. Qualifying a good contractor requires that you do your homework. The ROC has made this part of your job so much easier. Among the many resources found on the ROC's website, you'll find the "search for a contractor" link. This is where you'll want to be.

If you do find a prospective contractor, you will be able to go to the contractor's detail page. There will be more than enough information to teach you all you'll need to know.

What should you look for?

First things first, verify that their ROC number is current and valid. I do not recommend hiring anyone to do construction work, who isn't licensed.

Next, look for the contractor's name and phone number. You will also want to find the name of the qualifying party. This is the person who is ultimately responsible for all activities of the company.

Make sure that the person you're reviewing is the same person at the ROC site. Some unscrupulous people have used other people's ROC numbers. Be careful and be sure to report anything that seems suspicious to the ROC.

Next, look to the contractor's 'class and type'. This will tell you what kinds of work this contractor is licensed to do. The ROC lists a 'class and types' on their website. Look it up and verify that their license allows them to do the work you need done.

After that you want to review any complaints the contractor had filed against them. Keep in mind that we are all human and we all make mistakes. One or two minor problems shouldn't be enough to cross them off. However, a pattern of problems could be.

On this page you should also find information about filing a complaint. As well as how to make a claim against a contractor's bond.

Hopefully, you won't need to use this information. But in the case that you do, it's good to know where it is.

The ROC site isn't a ratings and review site. You will only find facts regarding the contractor's license history. Use this information to further narrow down your list.

Reviews and ratings

By now you have probably crossed a few, or even a lot of names off of your list. Which is exactly the point of this exercise. You want to narrow down your search to the very few contractors that you find best suited to for your project.

Companies tend to take on the personalities of their leadership. And like any other relationship, some people just get along better with certain personalities, while other kinds of personalities rub them the wrong way. That's just a fact of life.

In this step, you will be learning more about the personality of the contractor's company. I am very confident that you will cross off a few more names during this step in the process. That is a good thing too. The goal here to end up with ONE contractor that you actually hire.

Thanks to the Internet you can learn more about a contractor (or any business) faster than ever before. By visiting good reviews and ratings sites, you don't allow companies' control over their reviews and ratings. You can learn how they do business, how they treat their customers, and get a very good feel for the personality type of the contractor and their company.

I believe this is a far more effective way of learning about a contractor, than asking them for five or ten references. After all, what contractor isn't going to give you their very best references?

Can you imagine a contractor saying, "Oh yes, I can give you ten great references and ten very bad ones." I am sure that you can't. As a matter of fact, I know contractors are very selective about who they put on their "reference list". Their end goal is to close the deal and get a contract with you. A reference list is part of their marketing effort toward that end.

Some sites like Yelp, Manta, Angie's list, the BBB, and Rip-off Reports are a great place to start. There are so many more out there. Look for sites that do not allow the business to remove or alter their reviews or ratings.

As you read through the reviews and ratings, look for patterns of behavior. Good or bad. Perhaps one contractor has several complaints about up charges. Or another seems to be late on starting jobs. Or others are very defensive in their replies to complaints.

Use your own brain when reading through complaints. Some people will always find something to complain about. Look for legitimate complaints. And more importantly, pay attention to how the contractor responded to them. Ask yourself if that is the kind of person with whom you want to do business.

We are all human beings and we all make mistakes. If you are looking for the perfect contractor, they don't exist. The very best of us can and do make mistakes. Keep that in mind while reading through reviews and ratings.

As you read through reviews and ratings, and start to get a good feel for the kind of contractors they are, start making decisions about who you will be crossing off the list. Take your time, this is very important.

Some of the more popular ratings and reviews sites:

www.Yelp.com

www.Manta.com

www.Angieslist.com

www.Tofixit.com

There are many more sites in addition to these. Be sure that the sites you are using do not allow contractors to edit, or pay to have their reviews and ratings altered. Also watch out for "lead" sites, that offer to find a contractor for you. They make a living selling leads.

Interviewing the contractor

Many of those "free reports" will tell you to ask a contractor questions that we have already answered during this process. By reading the ROC's contractor details page, and looking at their reviews and ratings you have been able to narrow down your list without spending any time on the phone. Until now.

There are some very good reasons to call and interview a contractor before inviting them to bid on your project.

To get a good feel for their real life professionalism, in the way that they handle a phone call. If they answer that is, if not you will learn how prompt they are at returning your call.

You will be able to get the answers to questions that you did not get already. Such as questions about insurance and sub-contractors.

Use your "contractor interview" worksheet to help you conduct your interview. Always be polite, friendly and courteous. These should be friendly conversations, not interrogations. You're learning about the contractor, not drilling them on the finer points of their business.

Some contractors, believe it or not, won't like being bothered with any questions at all. They might say something like, **"Would you like us to come out and look at your roof"** or **"when you are ready, give us a call."** Don't be too shocked when you get that kind of dismissive comment. Explain that you have not decided who to invite to bid your project yet. If they still are resistant about answering your questions, then perhaps you may consider crossing them off of the list.

Introduce yourself: **"Hi, my name is (name) and I live in (City). Do you service my area?"**

If the answer is yes, and you know what kind of roof you have: **"Do you have experience with (your kind of roof)?"**

If the answer is yes, then ask, **"Are you insured? Both general liability and worker's compensation?"** I have written a section on insurance that you will be reading soon. For now, you are looking for a **"yes"** to both questions.

Arizona does not require a contractor to carry general liability insurance. However, Arizona does require a contractor to carry worker's compensation insurance. Unless the contractor is an owner operator. Some contractors may use a labor service that covers their employees' worker's compensation. Read the section on insurance for more information.

Next, ask, **"Do you use sub-contractors? And do they carry general liability and worker's compensation insurance?"**

Many contractors use sub-contractors to do the labor portion of their projects. There is nothing wrong with that practice, as long as they use professional sub-contractors.

If they do use sub-contractors you will want to know who they are, and get their ROC number as well. If they will be at your home, you have the right to know who they are. You might find some resistance to this question. But that's ok, many contractors won't be used to a homeowner asking such thorough questions.

Next, ask, **"How do you supervise your jobs?"** There are many ways contractors oversee their projects. What is important here is that they have some system in place to oversee their projects. You don't want a crew or sub-contractors left at your home unsupervised.

This question is a vital one: ***"Do you follow the manufacturer's instructions and specifications when installing a roof?"*** While it may seem reasonable to believe that all contractors do, I am here to tell you not all of them even bother reading the manufacturer's instructions. They just do whatever it is they have been doing for years.

At this point I would say that any contractor who does not feel it is vital to know and follow the manufacturer's instructions and specifications would never work on my own house. Accept no answer other than, ***"Yes."***.

Next, ask, ***"Do you provide a written labor warranty and materials warranty?"*** Arizona holds a licensed contractor responsible for their work for two years. After that you cannot file a complaint against them, or make a claim on their bond. Now, I am not a lawyer and this is not legal advice. If you have legal questions consult with an attorney.

Back to the vital importance of following the manufacturer's instructions and specifications if your contractor does

not. Then your roof materials will not be covered by the manufacturer's warranty. We will talk more about this in the section on "warranties".

At the end of your "interviewing the contractor" worksheet you have an area to make your comments. Write down anything about that contractor that you believe is worth noting. Carefully review all your information up to this point. You should have three or four names by now.

Insurance

Insurance is very important, as it protects everyone involved. If you have specific questions about an insurance contract, ask an insurance agent who specializes in business coverage.

General Liability Insurance

"Insurance policy that covers claims arising from a liability due to damage or injury (caused by negligence or acts of omission) during performance of his or her duties or business."

http://www.businessdictionary.com/definition/general-liability-insurance.html

Contractors in Arizona are not required by law to carry General Liability insurance. Although, I would not recommend hiring a contractor who does not carry it. It shows that they care about their customers enough to protect them. It also shows they are wise business people, in protecting themselves.

Worker's Compensation

"Financial support system established under law to provide income, medical care, and rehabilitation to employees for illness, injury, or death arising out of, and in the course of, their employment whether or not the employee was at fault. These benefits are claimed by the employees (or their dependents) as a matter of right and the employer cannot resort to any legal defense. Amount paid as a compensation is based on the salary of the employee (also on the number of his or her dependents in some jurisdictions) and is usually a specified maximum."
http://www.businessdictionary.com/definition/workerscompensation.html#ixzz3z3A8ST1U

Workers compensation is required by law. A person at the Arizona Industrial Commission told me, "If they have even one part-time employee, they are supposed to be covered." The exceptions to the rule are owner operator contractors. An owner is not required by law to cover themselves. Usually, they will have some other insurance to protect them.

Some contractors will hire their workers through an employment agency. The agency covers their employees for them.

This law applies to the Sub Contractors as well.

Special funds

You might be surprised to learn that Arizona has a special fund set aside; managed by the

Arizona Industrial Commission. This fund works in the same way as worker's compensation insurance, when an employee of an uninsured employer is injured. The injured worker only needs to go to the emergency and room and tell them that they were injured on the job. The hospital will begin the process.

The employer has no say in the matter. The employer cannot deny care to an injured worker, nor does the employee need that employer's consent to go to the emergency room. Should the employee be paid a claim through the special fund, the Arizona Industrial Commission will then go after that employer for the money paid, as well as any applicable fees and fines. It is illegal not to carry worker's compensation insurance if you are an employer in Arizona.

Ask your homeowner's agent

Before you start the work talk with your own homeowner's insurance agent. Tell them what you are doing, and ask them what your own policy covers should there be a problem. Also, ask if you might see a discount for having a new roof installed.

Who is the Industrial Commission of Arizona?

I felt it was important to talk a little more about who the Industrial Commission of Arizona is, and what they have to do with your roofing project. Most people, including contractors are unaware of who and what this organization is – but you won't be one of those people.

The Industrial Commission of Arizona offers many services, but for the purposes of this book they are the governing body that oversees worker's compensation in Arizona. Anything to do with worker's compensation goes through them.

If a contractor has a worker's compensation policy in place, they will be recorded by the Industrial Commission of Arizona and you can go look them up.

Go to:

www.ica.state.az.us

In the lower middle section of their home page, will see several blue tabs. Click on either "Resources for employers" or "Resources for medical providers". Look for the "search for worker's compensation insurance coverage" link in the list. Click it.

Then follow their directions to look up any contractor to verify they have a workman's compensation policy.

Keep in mind that ab owner/operator is not required to have one if they work alone. And some contractors will use an employment agency that covers their employees.

Invitation to bid

Now that you have finally narrowed down your list to a few contractors that you feel good about, it's time to send out an invitation to bid.

An invitation to bid is a document that tells the selected contractors what you want done, when you want it done, and what to expect from you should they be awarded the contract.

I recommend sending a friendly email, this way you will have started to build a "paper trail". Since we have moved past the narrowing down the list part of this process, I will be talking more about managing the project. This includes documenting EVERYTHING. From the invitation to bid, to the final walk through and everything in between.

What do you say? You can send them an email saying something like:

"HI,

My name is (name), we spoke with your company not too long about our roof in (city). We are interested in receiving a bid from your company to replace our roof.

In the spirit of transparency, I would like to be up front about what we will expect from you, should you be selected for the project.

- *The work will be done in accordance with the manufacturer's instructions and specifications.*
- *I will expect a pre-construction meeting with the person who sold me the project, and whoever will be in charge of the job.*
- *I would like to be given day to day progress reports.*
- *I will expect a final walk through, with the same persons in attendance as in the pre-construction meeting.*
- *I will expect a lien waiver for any payments that I make to your company.*

I also understand that you are in business to make a profit and I will make payments as agreed to, should you be selected as my contractor for this project.

If this is all acceptable then let's set up an appointment for you to come out."

Making the appointment(s)

When you make appointments with contractors, do them a favor and don't have them all showing up at once. No need to add any potential stress to the situation. Make sure each contractor has ample time to do their inspection, make their measurements and prepare a proposal for you.

BEWARE! Sales people in the construction industry usually get paid on commission. Watch for the pushy sales person who wants a decision now. Make it very clear to them that you will not be deciding during that meeting, and you are going to take your time to review their proposal on your own time.

Once the contractor has finished with their presentation, thank them for their time and let them know that you will be in touch one way or the other, soon.

Reading the proposals

Apples to apples

As a roof consultant I provide my clients with a detailed scope of work. This scope of work is used when inviting contractors to bid on a project, to assure that we are receiving "apples to apples" bids. In this case you have told them you expect that the work will be done in accordance with the manufacturer's instructions and specifications.

The scope of work

Each contractor should have named the brand name of materials they intend to use. If not, then you will want to ask them. Visit the manufacturer's website and compare their proposal to the manufacturer's installation instructions and specifications.

The minimum elements of a contract

I re-wrote this section three times! My thought initially was that I needed to explain what each element was. However, as I read though it I realized it was just confusing and wordy. So I decided to create a checklist instead. Use this checklist when reading though the proposals and make sure everything is there.

Minimum Elements of a contract checklist

To learn more, visit the ROC's website.

[__] 1. The name of the contractor and the contractor's business address and license number.

[__] 2. The name and mailing address of the owner and the jobsite address or legal description.

[__] 3. The date the parties entered into the contract.

[__] 4. The estimated date of completion of all work to be performed under the contract.

[__] 5. A description of the work to be performed under the contract.

[__] 6. The total dollar amount to be paid to the contractor by the owner for all work to be performed under the contract, including all applicable taxes.

[__] 7. The dollar amount of any advance deposit paid or scheduled to be paid to the contractor by the owner.

[__] 8. The dollar amount of any progress payment and the stage of construction at which the contractor will be entitled to collect progress payments during the course of construction under the contract.

[__] 9. That the property owner has the right to file a written complaint with the registrar for an alleged violation of section 32-1154, subsection A. The contract shall contain the registrar's telephone number and website address and shall state that complaints must be made within the applicable time period as set forth in section 32-1155, subsection A. The information in this paragraph must be prominently displayed in the contract in at least ten-point bold type, and the contract shall be signed by the property owner and the contractor or the contractor's designated representative. This paragraph does not apply to a person who is subject to and complies with section 12-1365.

C. At the time of signing a contract the owner shall be provided a legible copy of all documents signed and a written and signed receipt for and in the true amount of any cash paid to the contractor by the owner.

D. The requirements of this section shall not constitute prerequisites to the formation or enforcement of a contract. Failure to comply with the requirements of this section shall not constitute a defense by either party to an action for compensation, damages, breach, enforcement or other cause of action based on the contract.

Payment terms

I am going to say this over and over in this book. Never pay cash, always pay using a check or cashier's check. Always make copies of any payments, and include them in your job folder. Always get a signed lien waiver for any payments that you make to the contractor.

The down payment. There are many schools of thought on this issue. Some say don't make any down payment at all, and others say only make a small down payment. The fact is that some contractors need that money to buy materials. Others do not. The contractors that you are dealing with now, have been thoroughly researched by you yourself. It's really a matter of trust at this point.

As a contractor I have always asked for down payments. I have never run off with anyone's money. Contractors asking for a down payment is common. Do what you feel comfortable doing, and use your own common sense. If you have legal questions, I recommend that you contact and attorney.

Hidden damage!

Often when re-roofing we find "hidden damages," things that we can't see until we remove the existing roofing materials. It's very hard to estimate the total "hidden damages".

Your contract should talk about the cost of various hidden damages. There should be additional unit charges for "hidden damages". If you don't see this in their proposal you should email the contractor and ask. The reason I recommend sending an email, is that you keep a fully documented paper trail.

Change orders

Most contractors will have a limit on the amount of "hidden damage" charges before they require a signed change order agreement. Or you decide to make up grades to the work. This would also require a signed change order.

A change order will list the additional scope of work, and the cost for that work. Both you and the contractor (or their representative) need to sign it. Make sure that you get a copy and include it in your job folder.

Always use a check or cashier's check when making any payment. Always make copies of the payments and get a signed lien waiver for the amount of any payment that you make. Keep all copies in your job job folder.

Let's go back the minimum elements checklist and look closely at number nine.

"That the property owner has the right to file a written complaint with the registrar for an alleged violation of section 32-1154, subsection A. The contract shall contain the registrar's telephone number and website address and shall state that complaints must be made within the applicable time period as set forth in section 32-1155, subsection A. The information in this paragraph must be prominently displayed in the contract in at least ten-point bold type, and the contract shall be signed by the property owner and the contractor or the contractor's designated representative. This paragraph does not apply to a person who is subject to and complies with section 12-1365."

Notice how specific the ROC is about this one. They tell the contractor exactly what to say right down to the font size. They don't want them hiding this in the small print. There is no excuse for any contractor not having this in their contract. If you don't see it, you may want to ask the contractor about it. It could be that they have not updated their contracts in many years.

Workmanship standards

http://www.azroc.gov/Acrobat/Public/Workmanship_Standards.pdf

Warranties

Let's start by discussing the "labor warranty". The contractor's promise that the materials are going to be installed correctly. All licensed contractors in Arizona are held to a standard of workmanship.

Http://www.azroc.gov/Acrobat/public/Workmanship_Standards.pdf

Contractors are held to these standards by Arizona. If the contractor is doing their work as instructed by the manufacturer, most of the time the work will exceed standards.

Arizona holds the contractor responsible for their work for two years. You have the right to file a complaint, or bond claim within the first two years of the completion of the work, if the contractor is not willing to work with you.

The Arizona workmanship standards are used to determine if the contractor's work was to standard or not. Keep in mind that I am not an attorney. This is not taken as legal advice. If you do have a problem that cannot get resolved, please seek proper legal advice.

Or contact the ROC if you are still within the two year limit.

Materials Warranty

All manufacturers have some kind of limited warranty on their materials, which will cover defects in the materials resulting from their manufacturing process. These warranties can be very limited and they don't often include any labor cost.

Manufacturers will also have some kind of specifications and/or installation instructions that a contractor must follow, for their warranty to be valid. They won't warranty material that is installed incorrectly. And can you really blame them?

Many manufacturers also prorate their coverage based on expected service life of the materials. The value becoming less each year, until it reaches zero.

BEFORE you even hire a contractor, you should know what brand of materials that he intends to use. Find the manufacturer online and read their warranties' coverages and requirements. Some manufacturers have different levels of warranty coverages as well, if you use one of their certified contractors. Some will even offer labor and materials, if you upgrade.

Go to the manufacturer's website, and read the warranty information for the product that your contractor is proposing to install.

When the job is completed, you should receive the manufacturer's warranty documents from the contractor. Some manufacturers require you or your contractor to register your warranty at their website. If that is the case make sure it is done, and always keep copies of your warranty documents, your contract with the contractor and proof of payments in your job folder.

Let me say this in closing, if you hired a good contractor and they did their work correctly, chances are very good that you won't have any problems, and if there is an actual defect in materials. Manufacturers are actually pretty good about taking care of you. Just be sure that you go into this knowing exactly what your warranty coverages are, how to file a claim and what your own responsibility is.

Selecting and hiring your contractor

Before you hire your contractor read the sections on Lien waivers and Money. Just after this section.

It's time to make a decision, who's going to get your hard earned money. Not an easy one to make, since you've done your homework so well that all your proposals should be quite impressive.

When you are making your decision, try not to base it all on price alone; while that is certainly an important consideration, do not make it the only one. Other criteria include completeness of the proposal, level of professionalism and gut feeling.

Documentation

Send a "you're hired" email to the contractor. Type in "you're hired" in the subject line, to get their attention.

Pretty much repeat your invitation bid email with a few small changes.

"Hi,

My name is _____(you),_____ we live at __(address)_____. and _____(sales rep)_____presented me/us with a proposal recently.

I am interested in hiring your company.

In the spirit of fairness and transparency I want to make sure that you understand my expectations from a contractor.

- *Work will be done in accordance with the manufacturer's specifications and instructions.*
- *I will expect a pre-construction meeting with the person who sold me the job, the supervisor who will be overseeing my job as well as myself (and my spouse).*
- *I like to be kept informed throughout the project by email day to day.*
- *I will expect a final walk through.*
- *I will expect a lien waiver for every payment that I make to your company.*

I also understand that you are in business to make a profit and I will make payments to you as we agree.

If these expectations are agreeable to you, then let's move forward and set up an appointment for you to come out and visit with me/us."

If your contractor requires a down payment, get a lien waiver from them for the amount of the down payment. Print your emails from the invitation to bid, to the you're hired email, as well as their replies. Place those documents in your job folder along with a copy of the signed contract and your lien waiver.

Mechanic's liens

What is a lien?

In scary terms a lien is the most powerful tool a contractor has, to get money out of you. It's relatively simple to do, and very hard to get rid of. If you end up with a lien on your house, you may not be able to get it off without paying the contractor.

The bottom line here is <u>NOT</u> to allow a lien to be placed against your house. You can assure this by following the "rules of the money" -- always pay with a check or cashier's check. Always make copies of your payments. Always get a signed lien waiver from the contractor for any amount that you paid them.

Arizona Revised Statutes (A.R.S.) SS33-981-1006

The Rules of Money

The money

Don't play games with your hard earned money! Follow these rules regarding payments to any contractor.

1. NEVER PAY IN CASH! Always pay with a check or cashier's check.

2. Always write into the memo line of your payment exactly what the payment is for. *"Down payment"* or *"Progress payment"* or *"Change order"* or *"Final payment"* or whatever the payment is for.

3. Always make photos copies, front and back, of every payment and place them in your job folder.

4. Always get a signed lien waiver for any payments that you make to the contractor. And when you make the final payment make sure you get a final lien waver.

Don't play games with your money. Make the payments to your contractor as you agreed to in your contract with them. At the same time make sure that you do your due diligence to protect yourself.

Permits

A permit may be required by your city in order to do your project. Typically, the contractor is responsible for obtaining the necessary permits. However, if you are not sure please do call your city and ask.

You may also need to get permission from your HOA. That task is usually left up to the homeowner to take care of.

Make sure that you find out, and get whatever permits that you need.

Managing your project

Proper planning prevents poor production

You are the person writing the check. That makes you the boss. And while I don't recommend you hover over the workers, or pester the contractor unnecessarily, I do recommend that you pay attention and make sure the contractor knows that you are paying attention.

This should be done professionally and respectfully. Everyone involved on the project, from the contractor and his workers and of course you wants the job to go as smoothly as possible. The contractor wants to get paid and you want to get what you are paying for.

Pre-construction meeting

Do not overlook this very important part of the project's success. It won't take too long and it will set the mood for the rest of the job. At the end of the meeting everyone will be on the same page and your contractor will respect you for it. It's the professional way to do things.

Who should be there?

You of course and your spouse or significant other.

The person who sold you the job. And the person in charge of the project.

What will you discuss?

Go over the scope of work again line by line. I know that you have already read the scope of work and discussed it with your contractor. You have already compared it to the manufacturer's insulation instructions. The difference now is that the person who will actually be supervising the work is there, and don't assume they know the scope of work.

When will materials be delivered?

And where will they be stored? These are the two great questions to ask. If you are not happy with their suggestions then make your own. It's your home after all. You have every right to decide where materials will be stored.

How will they manage their waste?

If they are using a placed "roll off" dumpster, make sure you are aware of their intended location. Most of the time the contractor will want it in your driveway as close to the house as possible. This makes it easier for the crew to toss debris from the roof directly into the dumpster. If they are using a dump truck, then be sure you let them know where they can and cannot not drive it. Mostly I would say "keep it off the lawn."

How will they protect your property, you and themselves?

Every good contractor will have a safety program. Often they are implied and unwritten. What is important is that they have a good plan to protect your property and the people at your home, including themselves.

When will the work begin?

What is their start time and finish time each day? If you can get a solid date that would be great. Sometimes that's not easy, considering the nature of this work. It's very weather dependent as you can imagine. Get as close to a date as you can, at the very least something like "next Wednesday or Thursday" or whatever day is feasible. This gives you the opportunity to be prepared as well.

How long will the job take?

As a contractor I always answered the question, "Well, usually this kind of job will take us three to four days. Of course that depends on the weather and so on. But I will keep you informed as we move along." You should not hold a contractor to a hard completion date. You do want to make sure the work is done correctly, however, you don't want workers lingering around your house making noise, any longer than needed.

Will they work on weekends?

I always worked on weekends in my younger days, it was about making all the money back then. Not because I was greedy, but because I was so danged poor. I had to work the weekends. Later in my life though when I had a family, I decided not to work weekends anymore. And perhaps you don't want workers at your house on the weekend. It's up to you.

Who is the contact person during the work?

Some contractors give the supervisor or superintendent enough authority to handle any problems that may arise. Others don't. Be sure to ask and get their name and phone number.

This person should be the one you talk to about change orders. Hidden damages. Day to day questions or concerns. Or after-hours emergencies.

Where do the workers use the bathroom?

I know this sounds a little silly to ask, but you would not believe how many roofers will just hop down off the roof, find a nice corner in your back yard and relieve themselves. As a matter of fact, when I was reading Yelp reviews researching for this book, I read several complaints about that very thing. I would not recommend allowing them to use your bathroom. Of course this is up to you, but do you really want strangers wandering through your house? Make sure they have a plan for this, and won't be urinating in your yard.

How will they leave the house at the end of the day?

Will they clean up each day and make sure there are no debris on the ground? That the materials and debris on the roof are secured? Will they leave your home clean, organized, and safe?

Do they allow their workers to smoke?

Let me make this clear and I will be very blunt about this. NEVER allow smoking on the roof, or anywhere near the roofing debris. It is very dangerous! No good contractor would ever do that, but still make sure. I would suggest that you are very clear with them that there is to be no smoking on your roof or your property. Too many things can go wrong too fast.

I want to share a story with you. Many years ago, I was re-roofing an old house and ran off to the store for a snack. I left one worker behind to keep loading the roof. When I came back, I saw smoke pouring out of the roof. "What's happened?" He shrugged and said, "I don't know." I scrambled up the ladder and scaffolding, ripped off some decking with my bare hands and jumped into the attic. The insulation was on fire! "Get me some water!" As I was trying to snuff out the fire with my hands, he makes it up the ladder with a gallon of water and pours it on the flames, putting it out.

"Dude, I told you not to smoke on the roof." He swears, "I didn't, it wasn't me, man." I was shocked that he denied it. "You are the only one here, dude." I had to repaint the homeowner's ceiling because the water damaged it. And yes, I fired that guy. **NO SMOKING ON THE JOB!**

Be sure to use your pre-construction worksheet, and put it in your job folder when the meeting is over.

Checking the materials

Make sure your contractor lets you know when the materials are scheduled to be delivered. Most of the time, materials are delivered in the cable guy style, between x time and x time. Let the contractor know you will be inspecting the materials before any construction can begin. They will accommodate you so that they can get started on the work and make their money.

If the contractor has ordered a rooftop delivery, ask that they leave one of each item on the ground, for your inspection. For example, one bundle of shingles and a roll of base sheet. Or a tile and the peel and stick. Whatever the case may be, so that you can look at the materials close up with your own eyes.

I do not recommend anyone climbing on the roof unless you know what you are doing. It is very dangerous and you can get hurt if you slip. If you choose to climb onto the roof, you need to be absolutely sure what you are doing. Do not take the UN-necessary risk.

Make sure the materials are new, in good condition and the brand that was named in your contract. Verify the correct quantity was delivered and take photos. Make your notes on the materials check worksheet and include it along with your photos in the job folder.

If you have any questions about the materials, ask them NOW! Don't let the contractor start work if you are not sure about something regarding the materials. Always address any concerns or questions that come up during the work, immediately. It's not fair to spring this kind of thing on the contractor after the fact. They don't like that anymore than you would like getting a surprise change at the end of a job.

Day to day progress reports

Remember that you are the one paying the bill. And that ultimately makes you the boss. Treat your contractor with the same respect with which you would have them treat you. However, you need to stay on top of your project and your contractor needs to know that you are paying attention.

Make your own notes and take photos each day. Take photos of the work, your landscape, the trucks. Whatever is going on, document it.

This may seem like a lot of work, but in the case that there is a problem you will be very glad that you have documentation.

This practice also adds a level of accountability that many contractors are not used to having. Keeping them aware that you are paying attention will certainly keep them on their toes.

You might also want to ask the contractor(or their representative) to send you an update email at the end of each day. Ask them to tell you:

- What was done today
- What will they do tomorrow
- Did anyone get injured?
- Were there any unexpected damages uncovered?
- And anything else the contractor feels is relevant

Be sure to print a copy of each email, and any photos for your job folder. Always date the documents for quick reference.

The final walk through

The final walk through is the last and final chance that you have to make sure that the job is done correctly, before you write that last check. Make sure your contractor understands that you will expect a final walk through.

Who should be there?

- You and your spouse of significant other
- The person who sold you the job
- The person in charge of the project

What will you be looking for?

Since you have been paying close attention to the work throughout the project's progress, you already have a pretty good idea if the project is done right or not. I suspect if you don't believe that it has been done right you wouldn't be doing a final walk through.

- Is your yard clean?
- Is any of your property damaged?
- Are all of the extra materials removed or stored properly?
- Are any dumpsters or trucks gone?
- Do you have your warranty paperwork?
- Was the work completed as agreed?

Use the "final walk through form" in this book to help guide you through the process. If you do find issues that you would like corrected before you write the final check, be sure that you write them down on the "punch list" portion of the "final walk through form" and ask the contractor to take care of them.

IMPORTANT! When you make your final payment always get a signed lien waiver, as well as a PAID IN FULL receipt. And place those documents in your job folder.

Handling a problem

Many years ago someone told me "you can tell who the true professionals are by how they handle things when they are going wrong. Anyone can look good when things are going right."

It's a fact of life that things will go wrong. Not one of us is perfect, we all make mistakes. For all the planning and preparation that we do, something can still go wrong, and we will need to handle the problem correctly.

Keep in mind that we are human beings with emotions, you and the contractor alike have feelings. Try to remain respectful and that will go a long way toward solving a problem. Always address any problems right away. The contractor will appreciate it and it's not very fair to spring it on him at the last minute.

Believe me, if there is a problem your contractor will want to know as soon as possible. The sooner they know about the problem, the easier it is to resolve it. Waiting until the project is done, is the worst way to handle a problem.

The first thing that you will need to do is to document the problem. Make some notes, take a few photos and then email your contractor. Always print any emails and put the copy in your job folder.

Allow your contractor to respond and find a solution to whatever the problem is. Most of the time, they will deal with a problem very quickly. They want to finish up and get paid after all.

So what do you do if the contractor refuses or ignores your concerns? Well, that's a big problem. This is YOUR home! As a contractor myself, I can't imagine just ignoring someone's concerns.

Before you take any actions, consult with a trusted friend, relative or other person. Make sure your concerns are valid before you "stir up the pot". You might even call a roof consultant and ask a few questions.

Perhaps you don't need to validate your concern, it could be a very clear problem.

Either way, you will need to document the problem. If needed STOP THE WORK so that you can document the problem. It's your house and you can refuse access to the contractor. If the problem is severe, then you might consider hiring another contractor to tarp the area. Unless the problem is so bad that you have to have it repaired immediately, then do that. But be sure that you fully document the problem.

- What is the problem?
- When did you notify the contractor?
- When and what was their response?
- What was your action?
- Take lots of photos

You might even consider hiring a roof consultant to inspect and report on the problem, if you feel that it's that bad. The more that you can document the problem the better.

If you do involve any other contractors or a consultant, do them a favor and make sure your contractor is not there while they are. It's uncomfortable for everyone.

If after all this, the contractor is still not addressing your concerns you might want to consider filing a complaint with the ROC. You can find their complaint guidelines and forms on their website.

This is why you have been documenting the job, the ROC will want as much documentation as you can provide them.

Your other option would be to consult an attorney. I am not an attorney, so none of this is to be taken as legal advice. If you feel that you need legal advice, consult an attorney.

To summarize:

- Be respectful
- Allow the contractor to respond
- Validate your concerns
- Document everything
- However, since you have done your homework by using this book to find a good contractor, chances are pretty good that you won't ever find yourself in this situation.

THE END

Finding a contractor worksheet

How To Find, Hire, and Work with an Arizona Roofing Contractor

SOURCE	NAME	PHONE	Web Site	ROC#	ROC Review	Online ratings	Comments

C 2016

Contractor interview work sheet

Date: _____ Time: _____

Contractor name: _____Phone Number: _____
Did they answer? _____ If not, when did they call back Date: _____ Time: _____
Do have experience with my kind of roof?

_____

Are you insured?

_____

General Liability?

_____

Workman's compensation?

_____

How do you supervise your jobs?

_____

_____

_____

Do you use sub-contractors?

_____

What is their ROC number ?

_____

Are they insured?

_____

General Liability? _____
Workman's compensation? _____
Are you OK with a pre-construction meeting with me before starting the work ?

_____

Do you follow the manufacturer's specifications/instructions ?

_____

Do you offer a labor warranty, and for how long?

_____

Do you provide the manufacturer's warranty and register it with the manufacture?

_____

Comments:

_____

_____

_____

_____

_____

_____

_____

_____

_____

_____

_____

Minimum Elements of a contract checklist

To learn more, visit the ROC's website.

[__] 1. The name of the contractor and the contractor's business address and license number.

[__] 2. The name and mailing address of the owner and the jobsite address or legal description.

[__] 3. The date the parties entered into the contract.

[__] 4. The estimated date of completion of all work to be performed under the contract.

[__] 5. A description of the work to be performed under the contract.

[__] 6. The total dollar amount to be paid to the contractor by the owner for all work to be performed under the contract, including all applicable taxes.

[__] 7. The dollar amount of any advance deposit paid or scheduled to be paid to the contractor by the owner.

[__] 8. The dollar amount of any progress payment and the stage of construction at which the contractor will be entitled to collect progress payments during the course of construction under the contract.

[__] 9. That the property owner has the right to file a written complaint with the registrar for an alleged violation of section 32-1154, subsection A. The contract shall contain the registrar's telephone number and website address and shall state that complaints must be made within the applicable time period as set forth in section 32-1155, subsection A. The information in this paragraph must be prominently displayed in the contract in at least ten-point bold type, and the contract shall be signed by the property owner and the contractor or the contractor's designated representative. This paragraph does not apply to a person who is subject to and complies with section 12-1365.

Payment terms: _____

Hidden Charges/Change order terms: _____

Material warranty:_____ Labor warranty: _____

Reveiw scope of work to the manufacturer's installation instructions: _____

Pre construction meeting

Date: _____ Time: _____
Who attended the meeting:
_____
_____
_____

Reviewed the scope of work ?   YES   NO
Discuss materials delivery/storage:
_____
_____
_____

Discuss waist management:
_____
_____
_____

Safety concerns (property and persons):
_____
_____
_____

Work hours _____ am to _____ pm Work days S | M | T | W | Th | F | S

Contact on site name: _____ phone: _____
Contact off site name: _____ phone: _____
Emergency contact: _____ phone: _____
Company email:
_____
Restroom Policy: _____
(No one is to use the yard as a restroom)
End of day clean explications:
_____
_____
_____

NO SMOKING ON SITE ! This is not up for debate, the answer is NO. If anyone feels the need to smoke, they must leave the property to do so.
Additional comments:
_____
_____
_____
_____
_____
_____
_____
_____

Attendees initials | _____ | _____ | _____ | _____ | _____ | _____ C 2016

Is your yard clean? _____
_____
_____

Is any of your property damaged?_____
_____
_____

Are all of the extra materials removed or stored properly?_____
_____
_____

Are any dumpsters or trucks gone? _____
_____
_____

Do you have your warranty paperwork?_____
_____
_____

Was the work completed as agreed?_____
_____
_____

Comments_____
_____
_____
_____
_____
_____
_____
_____
_____
_____
_____

ARIZONA LIEN WAIVER AND RELEASE FORM
CONDITIONAL WAIVER AND RELEASE ON FINAL PAYMENT
(Pursuant to A.R.S. 33-1008)

Project: _____

Job No: _____

On reciept of the undersigned check from _____
(Maker of check) in the sum of $ _____ (Amount of
check) payable to

_____(Payee or Payees of check) and when the check
has been properly endorsed and has been paid by the bank on which it is drawn, this
document becomes effective to release any mechanic's lien, any state or federal statutory
bond right, any private bond right, any claim for payment and any rights under any similar
ordinance, rule or statute related to claim or payment rights for persons in the undersigned's
possition, the undersigned has on the of _____ (Owner)
located at _____
This release covers the final payment to the undersigned for all labor, services, equipment or
materials furnished to the jobsite or to the job site or to
_____ (Person with whom undersigned
contracted) except for the disputed claims in the amount of
$ _____. Before any recipient of this document relies on it, this
person should verify the evidence of payment to the undersigned.

The undersigned warrants that he either has already paid or will use the monies be receives
from this final payment to promptly pay in full all his laborers, sub-contractors, materialmen
and suppliers for all work, materials, equipment or services provided for or to the above
referenced project up to the date of this waiver.

Date: _____

_____
(Company Name)

By: _____
(Signature)

_____
(Title)

www.ingramcontent.com/pod-product-compliance
Lightning Source LLC
Chambersburg PA
CBHW051339200326
41519CB00026B/7479